EASY GRILLED CHEESE COOKBOOK

THE EFFORTLESS CHEF SERIES

VOL. #XXXIX

By
Chef Maggie Chow
Copyright © 2015 by Saxonberg
Associates

Published by
BookSumo, a division of Saxonberg
Associates
http://www.booksumo.com/

A GIFT FROM ME TO YOU...

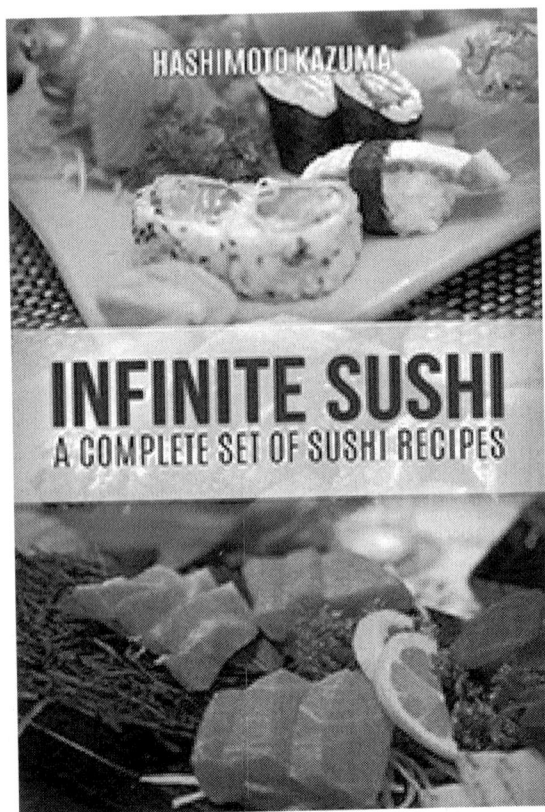

HASHIMOTO KAZUMA

INFINITE SUSHI
A COMPLETE SET OF SUSHI RECIPES

Send the Book!

I know you like easy cooking. But what about Japanese Sushi?

Join my private reader's club and get a copy of ***Infinite Sushi: A Complete Set of Sushi and Japanese Recipes*** by fellow BookSumo author Hashimoto Kazuma for FREE!

Send the Book!

Enjoy some of the best sushi available!

You will also receive updates about all my new books when they are free. So please show your support.

Also don't forget to like and subscribe on the social networks. I love meeting my readers. Links to all my profiles are below so please click and connect :)

Facebook

Twitter

ABOUT THE AUTHOR.

Maggie Chow is the author and creator of your favorite *Easy Cookbooks* and *The Effortless Chef Series*. Maggie is a lover of all things related to food. Maggie loves nothing more than finding new recipes, trying them out, and then making them her own, by adding or removing ingredients, tweaking cooking times, and anything to make the recipe not only taste better, but be easier to cook!

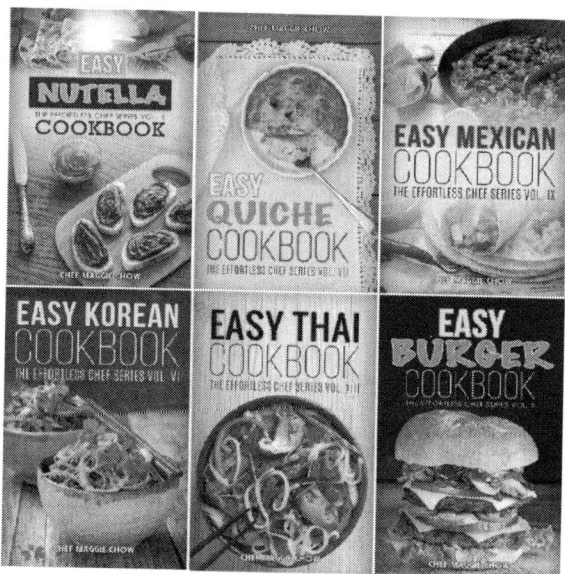

For a complete listing of all my books please see my author page.

INTRODUCTION

Welcome to *The Effortless Chef Series*!
Thank you for taking the time to
download the *Easy Grilled Cheese
Cookbook*. Come take a journey with me
into the delights of easy cooking. The
point of this cookbook and all my
cookbooks is to exemplify the effortless
nature of cooking simply.

In this book we focus on Grilled Cheese.
You will find that even though the
recipes are simple, the taste of the
dishes is quite amazing.

So will you join me in an adventure of
simple cooking? If the answer is yes
(and I hope it is) please consult the table
of contents to find the dishes you are
most interested in. Once you are ready
jump right in and start cooking.

— Chef Maggie Chow

TABLE OF CONTENTS

ANY ISSUES? CONTACT ME

If you find that something important to you is missing from this book please contact me at maggie@booksumo.com.

I will try my best to re-publish a revised copy taking your feedback into consideration and let you know when the book has been revised with you in mind.

:)

— Chef Maggie Chow

NOTICE TO PRINT READERS:

Hey, because you purchased the print version of this book you are entitled to its original digital version for free by Amazon.

So when you have the time, please review your purchases, and download the Kindle version of this book.

You might enjoy consuming this book more in its original digital format.

;)

But, in any case, take care and enjoy reading in whatever format you choose!

LEGAL NOTES

COMMON ABBREVIATIONS

cup(s)	C.
tablespoon	tbsp
teaspoon	tsp
ounce	oz
pound	lb

*All units used are standard American measurements

CHAPTER 1: EASY GRILLED CHEESE RECIPES

CLASSICAL AMERICAN GRILLED CHEESE

Ingredients

- 4 slices white bread
- 2 slices Cheddar cheese
- 3 tbsps butter, divided

Directions

- Get a frying pan hot with nonstick spray before doing anything else.
- Take one piece of bread and coat it with butter on one side. Lay the bread in the pan on the butter side. Then put a piece of cheese.
- Get another piece of bread and put butter on one side. Place this

slice over the cheese with its butter side facing up.

- Heat until both sides of the bread are nice and golden and the cheese has melted fully.
- Continue for all of your bread and cheese.
- Enjoy.

Servings: 2

Timing Information:

Preparation	Cooking	Total Time
5 mins	15 mins	20 mins

Nutritional Information:

Calories	400 kcal
Fat	28.3 g
Carbohydrates	25.7g
Protein	11.1 g
Cholesterol	76 mg
Sodium	639 mg

* Percent Daily Values are based on a 2,000 calorie diet.

ENHANCED TOMATO PESTO GRILLED CHEESE

Ingredients

- 2 slices Italian bread
- 1 tbsp softened butter, divided
- 1 tbsp prepared pesto sauce, divided
- 1 slice provolone cheese
- 2 slices tomato
- 1 slice American cheese

Directions

- Get a frying pan hot with nonstick spray before doing anything else.
- Take one piece of bread and coat it with butter on one side. Lay the bread in the pan on the butter side. Then put half of your pesto. Then a piece of provolone, then a piece of American, then your tomato, then the rest of the pesto.

- Get another piece of bread and coat one side with butter. Lay this piece with its butter side facing up on top of your pesto.
- Cook your sandwich for 6 mins each side until completely golden.
- Enjoy.

Servings: 1

Timing Information:

Preparation	Cooking	Total Time
5 mins	10 mins	15 mins

Nutritional Information:

Calories	503 kcal
Fat	36.5 g
Carbohydrates	24.2g
Protein	20.4 g
Cholesterol	82 mg
Sodium	1108 mg

* Percent Daily Values are based on a 2,000 calorie diet.

Oregano Mozzarella Grilled Cheese

Ingredients

- 1/4 C. unsalted butter
- 1/8 tsp garlic powder (optional)
- 12 slices white bread
- 1 tsp dried oregano
- 1 (8 oz) package shredded mozzarella cheese
- 1 (24 oz) jar vodka marinara sauce

Directions

- Turn on the broiler before doing anything else.
- Get a baking dish and lay half of your bread pieces.
- On top of each piece of bread put some mozzarella. Then top the cheese with the remaining pieces of bread.

- With a butter knife coat each sandwich with some butter. Then season the butter by applying some oregano and garlic powder.
- Broil for 4 mins then turn each sandwich and apply butter, oregano, and garlic to its opposite side. Broil for another 4 mins.
- Enjoy with the marinara as a dip.

Servings: 6

Timing Information:

Preparation	Cooking	Total Time
8 mins	7 mins	15 mins

Nutritional Information:

Calories	394 kcal
Fat	18.3 g
Carbohydrates	42g
Protein	15 g
Cholesterol	46 mg
Sodium	1032 mg

* Percent Daily Values are based on a 2,000 calorie diet.

CHEDDAR GRILLED CHEESES

Ingredients

- 18 slices bread
- 4 tbsps butter
- 9 slices Cheddar cheese

Directions

- Set your oven to 450 degrees before doing anything else.
- Coat one side of half your bread pieces with butter, and lay those sides facing downward, then put cheese, on each piece. Put some more butter on the other pieces of bread and place the slices on top of the cheese with the butter side facing upwards.
- Bake for 9 mins then flip, and bake for 5 more mins.
- Enjoy.

Servings: 9

Timing Information:

Preparation	Cooking	Total Time
10 mins	15 mins	25 mins

Nutritional Information:

Calories	293 kcal
Fat	16.2 g
Carbohydrates	25.7g
Protein	10.9 g
Cholesterol	43 mg
Sodium	553 mg

* Percent Daily Values are based on a 2,000 calorie diet.

TOMATO JALAPENO GRILLED CHEESE SANDWICH

Ingredients

- 2 tbsps butter or margarine
- 4 slices white bread
- 2 slices American cheese
- 1 roma (plum) tomato, thinly sliced
- 1/4 small onion, chopped
- 1 jalapeno pepper, chopped

Directions

- Get a frying hot with some nonstick spray before doing anything else.
- Take two pieces of bread and coat with butter. Put them in the pan with the buttered side facing down. Then add a piece of cheese to each. Then onions, then, tomato, then jalapeno.

- Top with remaining slices of bread. Put some more butter on the top of the sandwiches before you flip them.
- Cook until both sides are fully golden.
- Enjoy.

Servings: 2

Timing Information:

Preparation	Cooking	Total Time
2 mins	3 mins	5 mins

Nutritional Information:

Calories	352 kcal
Fat	22.1 g
Carbohydrates	28.2g
Protein	10.7 g
Cholesterol	57 mg
Sodium	846 mg

* Percent Daily Values are based on a 2,000 calorie diet.

GRILLED CHEESE WITH BACON I

Ingredients

- 8 slices bacon
- 1/4 C. butter, softened
- 8 slices white bread
- 8 slices American cheese
- 8 slices tomato

Directions

- Fry your bacon in a frying pan before continuing. Remove oil excess. Put bacon to the side.
- Butter 4 pieces of bread and place them in the pan with the butter side downwards. Add your cheese, then bacon, then more cheese, and finally 2 pieces of tomato.
- Top with remaining pieces of bread. Before flipping add butter to the top piece of bread.

- Brown both sides, and make sure your cheese is melted.
- Enjoy.

Servings: 4

Timing Information:

Preparation	Cooking	Total Time
10 mins	5 mins	15 mins

Nutritional Information:

Calories	557 kcal
Fat	38.7 g
Carbohydrates	28.6g
Protein	23.8 g
Cholesterol	104 mg
Sodium	1696 mg

* Percent Daily Values are based on a 2,000 calorie diet.

MAGGIE'S FAVORITE GRILLED CHEESE

Ingredients

- 8 (1 oz) slices bread
- 4 slices Cheddar cheese
- 1 large tomato, sliced
- 2 serrano peppers, seeded and thinly sliced
- 2 tsps dried basil
- salt and pepper to taste
- 2 tbsps butter

Directions

- Get a frying pan hot with nonstick spray before doing anything else.
- Butter half of your bread pieces and place them with the butter side downwards in the pan. Add cheese, then add some basil, then add some serrano slices, then

pepper, then 1 piece of tomato, then salt.

- Top your sandwiches with the remaining bread. Before flipping coat the new piece of bread with some butter.
- Cook for 4 mins per side. Make sure everything is browned nicely, then flip.
- Enjoy.

Servings: 4

Timing Information:

Preparation	Cooking	Total Time
10 mins	5 mins	15 mins

Nutritional Information:

Calories	327 kcal
Fat	17.1 g
Carbohydrates	31.3g
Protein	12 g
Cholesterol	45 mg
Sodium	703 mg

* Percent Daily Values are based on a 2,000 calorie diet.

PEPPERJACK GRILLED CHEESE

Ingredients

- 1 tbsp mayonnaise, divided
- 2 slices white bread
- 2 slices American cheese
- 1 slice pepper jack cheese

Directions

- Get a frying pan hot with nonstick spray.
- Coat half your bread pieces with mayo. Then put them into the frying pan with the mayo side facing downwards.
- Add your pepper jack cheese, then American cheese to each slice. Cover cheese with the rest of your bread. Finally coat the new slice of bread with mayo.
- Cook for 3 mins, then flip, then continue for another 3 mins.

- Enjoy.

Servings: 1

Timing Information:

Preparation	Cooking	Total Time
10 mins	5 mins	15 mins

Nutritional Information:

Calories	500 kcal
Fat	34.9 g
Carbohydrates	27.2g
Protein	19.5 g
Cholesterol	74 mg
Sodium	1349 mg

* Percent Daily Values are based on a 2,000 calorie diet.

GRILLED CHEESE WITH BACON II

Ingredients

- 2 slices cracked wheat bread
- 2 thin slices aged Cheddar cheese
- 2 slices Honey crisp apple, or more to taste
- 2 cooked bacon strips
- 2 tsps butter, or your preferred amount

Directions

- Get a frying pan hot with some nonstick spray.
- On a piece of bread layer: a piece of cheese, some bacon, a few slices of apple, and another piece of cheese. Top with another piece of bread.

- Coat one side of the sandwich with half your butter. Place this side facing down in the pan.
- Before flipping, coat the opposite with remaining butter.
- Cook until golden on all sides (4 mins per side).
- Enjoy.

Servings: 1

Timing Information:

Preparation	Cooking	Total Time
10 mins	5 mins	15 mins

Nutritional Information:

Calories	381 kcal
Fat	19.2 g
Carbohydrates	35.1g
Protein	18.4 g
Cholesterol	50 mg
Sodium	876 mg

* Percent Daily Values are based on a 2,000 calorie diet.

Rustic Grilled Cheese

(Apple, Ham, Sourdough)

Ingredients

- 1/4 C. finely chopped Granny Smith apple
- 1 tbsp finely chopped pecans
- 1 tbsp creamy salad dressing (such as Miracle Whip(R))
- 1 tbsp sour cream
- 8 slices Colby cheese
- 8 slices sourdough bread
- 4 thick slices ham
- 1/4 C. margarine

Directions

- Begin to preheat a skillet with some nonstick spray.
- Get a bowl mix: sour cream, apple, salad dressing, and pecans. Set to the side.

- Take half of your bread and layer the following on each slice: 1 piece of Colby, ham, another piece of Colby, one piece of bread.
- Coat the top of the sandwich with some margarine then fry them in the skillet for 3 mins per side.
- Once finished and golden put some pecan mix in the center of each sandwich.
- Enjoy.

Servings: 4

Timing Information:

Preparation	Cooking	Total Time
10 mins	5 mins	15 mins

Nutritional Information:

Calories	595 kcal
Fat	38.2 g
Carbohydrates	33.8g
Protein	29.2 g
Cholesterol	89 mg
Sodium	1569 mg

* Percent Daily Values are based on a 2,000 calorie diet.

MANGO GRILLED CHEESE

Ingredients

- 1/4 C. mango chutney
- 4 slices crusty bread, cut diagonally from a large loaf
- 6 slices black forest ham
- 4 slices white Cheddar cheese
- 2 tbsps butter, softened

Directions

- Get a frying pan hot with nonstick spray.
- Layer the following on two pieces of bread: mango chutney, 3 pieces of ham, 2 pieces of cheddar, and remaining pieces of bread.
- Coat the sandwich with butter on all sides.
- Fry for 4 mins per side.
- Enjoy.

Servings: 2

Timing Information:

Preparation	Cooking	Total Time
5 mins	5 mins	10 mins

Nutritional Information:

Calories	523 kcal
Fat	34.9 g
Carbohydrates	35.9g
Protein	17.9 g
Cholesterol	90 mg
Sodium	990 mg

* Percent Daily Values are based on a 2,000 calorie diet.

PARMIGIANO-REGGIANO CHEDDAR GRILLED CHEESE

Ingredients

- 1/4 C. butter, softened
- 1 C. freshly grated Parmigiano-Reggiano cheese
- 8 slices cooked bacon
- 4 slices Cheddar cheese
- 8 slices sourdough bread

Directions

- Get a bowl, evenly mix: parmesan, and butter.
- Get a frying hot with nonstick spray.
- Layer one piece of cheddar, and two pieces of bacon on half of your pieces of bread. Then put another piece of bread to form a sandwich. Coat sandwich with

butter parmesan mix on both sides.

- Cook for 4 mins per side.
- Enjoy.

Servings: 4

Timing Information:

Preparation	Cooking	Total Time
10 mins	6 mins	16 mins

Nutritional Information:

Calories	748 kcal
Fat	50.1 g
Carbohydrates	30.4g
Protein	43 g
Cholesterol	135 mg
Sodium	2211 mg

* Percent Daily Values are based on a 2,000 calorie diet.

EASY ITALIAN HERBED GRILLED CHEESE

Ingredients

- 1 tbsp butter, softened
- 2 slices bread
- 2 slices sharp Cheddar cheese
- 1 tbsp chopped parsley
- 1 tsp chopped basil
- 1 tsp oregano
- 1 tsp chopped fresh rosemary
- 1 tsp chopped fresh dill

Directions

- Get your frying hot with nonstick spray.
- Coat one side of half your pieces of bread with 1/2 a tbsp of butter.
- Place one slice of cheddar on each piece of bread, then add dill, rosemary, parsley, oregano, and basil. Top with remaining bread.

Use 1/2 tablespoon of butter to coat the top of each sandwich.

- Fry for 4 mins per side. Until cheese is fully melted.
- Enjoy.

Servings: 1

Timing Information:

Preparation	Cooking	Total Time
10 mins	6 mins	16 mins

Nutritional Information:

Calories	470 kcal
Fat	32.2 g
Carbohydrates	27.4g
Protein	18.4 g
Cholesterol	90 mg
Sodium	777 mg

* Percent Daily Values are based on a 2,000 calorie diet.

GOUDA, ARTICHOKE GRILLED CHEESE

Ingredients

- 2 tbsps grapeseed oil
- 1/2 red onion, thinly sliced
- 8 slices German rye bread
- salt and ground black pepper to taste
- 4 slices smoked Gouda cheese
- 4 slices provolone cheese
- 1/4 C. marinated artichoke hearts, drained and chopped

Directions

- Fry your onions for 10 mins in grapeseed oil. Then place to the side in a bowl.
- Coat your bread pieces with the oil remains from frying the onions and some pepper and salt.

- Place half of the bread pieces in the skillet with the oiled side facing downwards and layer: 1 piece of provolone, artichoke hearts, 1 piece of Gouda, and onion. Place remaining pieces of bread to form sandwiches.
- Fry sandwiches for 4 mins, then flip.
- Enjoy.

Servings: 4

Timing Information:

Preparation	Cooking	Total Time
15 mins	15 mins	30 mins

Nutritional Information:

Calories	437 kcal
Fat	24.6 g
Carbohydrates	34.3g
Protein	20.1 g
Cholesterol	51 mg
Sodium	1028 mg

* Percent Daily Values are based on a 2,000 calorie diet.

FETA AND ONION GRILLED CHEESE

Ingredients

- 1 1/2 tsps butter, softened
- 2 slices whole wheat bread, or your favorite bread
- 2 tbsps crumbled feta cheese
- 2 slices Cheddar cheese
- 1 tbsp chopped red onion
- 1/4 tomato, thinly sliced

Directions

- Get a frying pan hot with nonstick spray.
- Coat one side of half of your bread pieces. Place them into the pan then layer: cheddar, red onions, feta, and tomatoes.
- Top with remaining bread pieces, and coat the bread with butter.

- Cook for 4 mins per side, until cheese fully melted.
- Enjoy.

Servings: 1

Timing Information:

Preparation	Cooking	Total Time
5 mins	5 mins	10 mins

Nutritional Information:

Calories	482 kcal
Fat	30.9 g
Carbohydrates	27.1g
Protein	24.6 g
Cholesterol	92 mg
Sodium	876 mg

* Percent Daily Values are based on a 2,000 calorie diet.

Easy Cheddar and Muenster Grilled Cheese

Ingredients

- 2 tsps butter
- 1 slice Cheddar cheese
- 1 slice Muenster cheese
- 1 slice provolone cheese
- 2 slices rye bread

Directions

- Set the broiler in your oven to low preferably before doing anything else.
- Take all of your bread pieces and coat them with butter. Layer Muenster and cheddar on the non-buttered side of each piece of bread. Place everything on a baking sheet.
- Broil everything until the cheese starts to bubble. Remove the

baking dish from the broiler and press two pieces of bread together to form sandwiches.

Servings: 1

Timing Information:

Preparation	Cooking	Total Time
3 mins	6 mins	9 mins

Nutritional Information:

Calories	555 kcal
Fat	35.7 g
Carbohydrates	32.2g
Protein	26.5 g
Cholesterol	98 mg
Sodium	1082 mg

* Percent Daily Values are based on a 2,000 calorie diet.

GOAT GRILLED CHEESE

Ingredients

- 2 eggs, beaten
- 1 1/2 C. grated Romano cheese
- 1 (8 oz) package fresh chevre (goat) cheese
- 8 slices bread
- 8 slices tomato

Directions

- Get a bowl for only whisked eggs.
- Get a 2nd bowl for only parmesan.
- Take half of your bread pieces, and apply a layer of goat cheese. Then 2 tomato pieces. Top with another piece of bread to form a sandwich.
- Dip the sandwich into the eggs first, then into the parmesan. Make sure all sides are coated

evenly. Do this again until all bread has been formed into sandwiches.

- Cook your sandwiches in a frying pan coated with nonstick spray for 4 mins per side.
- Enjoy.

Servings: 4

Timing Information:

Preparation	Cooking	Total Time
20 mins	10 mins	30 mins

Nutritional Information:

Calories	558 kcal
Fat	33.2 g
Carbohydrates	30.7g
Protein	33.9 g
Cholesterol	184 mg
Sodium	1206 mg

* Percent Daily Values are based on a 2,000 calorie diet.

PEANUT BUTTER AMERICAN GRILLED CHEESE

Ingredients

- 2 slices bacon
- 1 tbsp smooth peanut butter
- 2 slices soft white bread
- 1 slice American cheese
- 1 tbsp butter, softened

Directions

- For 10 mins fry your bacon until crispy. Remove oil excesses.
- Take half of your pieces of bread and spread peanut butter, and then a layer a piece of cheese. Cover with the other bread pieces to form a sandwich.
- Fry for 4 mins per side in the same pan. Then flip.
- Enjoy.

Servings: 1

Timing Information:

Preparation	Cooking	Total Time
5 mins	20 mins	25 mins

Nutritional Information:

Calories	534 kcal
Fat	37.7 g
Carbohydrates	29.2g
Protein	21 g
Cholesterol	77 mg
Sodium	1335 mg

* Percent Daily Values are based on a 2,000 calorie diet.

GRILLED CREAM CHEESE

Ingredients

- 1 (3 oz) package cream cheese
- 3/4 C. mayonnaise
- 8 oz shredded Colby-Monterey Jack cheese
- 3/4 tsp garlic salt
- 8 slices French bread
- 2 tbsps butter

Directions

- Get a frying hot.
- Get bowl, evenly mix: salt, cream cheese, garlic, shredded cheese, and mayo.
- Layer half of your pieces of bread with the cream cheese mix. Then top with the remaining pieces of bread to form sandwiches.
- Coat the outside of each sandwich with butter.

- Cook for 4 mins per side until cheese fully melted.
- Enjoy.

Servings: 4

Timing Information:

Preparation	Cooking	Total Time
12 mins	8 mins	20 mins

Nutritional Information:

Calories	783 kcal
Fat	64.9 g
Carbohydrates	32g
Protein	20.6 g
Cholesterol	109 mg
Sodium	1436 mg

* Percent Daily Values are based on a 2,000 calorie diet.

SPICY SPANISH JALAPENO MONTEREY GRILLED CHEESE

Ingredients

- 2 oz cream cheese, softened
- 1 tbsp sour cream
- 10 pickled jalapeno pepper slices, or to taste - chopped
- 2 ciabatta sandwich rolls
- 4 tsps butter
- 8 tortilla chips, mashed
- 1/2 C. shredded Colby-Monterey Jack cheese

Directions

- Get a bowl, evenly mix: pickled jalapeno, cream cheese, and sour cream.
- Get your frying pan hot with nonstick spray.
- Cut your ciabattas in half horizontally. Then cut off the

round potion of each piece to make normal bread slices.

- Take half of the ciabatta pieces and layer, half of your cream cheese mix, then half of your Monterey, and half mashed chips. Form sandwiches with the remaining piece of bread. Repeat again to form another sandwich.
- Before frying coat the outside of the sandwiches with butter.
- Fry for 4 mins, until cheese is nicely melted.
- Enjoy.

Servings: 2

Timing Information:

Preparation	Cooking	Total Time
10 mins	10 mins	20 mins

Nutritional Information:

Calories	528 kcal
Fat	34 g
Carbohydrates	40.9g
Protein	16.5 g
Cholesterol	89 mg
Sodium	1121 mg

* Percent Daily Values are based on a 2,000 calorie diet.

GRILLED CHEESE WITH BACON
III

Ingredients

- 8 (3/4 inch thick) slices sourdough bread
- 1/4 C. butter
- 8 slices cooked thick bacon
- 8 slices pepper jack cheese
- 1 red onion, sliced and separated into rings
- 1 avocado, halved and cut into 1/4-inch slices

Directions

- Layer the following on half of your slices of bread: 1 piece of cheese, avocado pieces, 1 piece of cheese, onions.
- Top with remaining bread slices to form a sandwich. Coat the

outsides of the sandwich with butter.
- Fry for 4 mins on each side, until cheese melted.
- Enjoy.

.

Servings: 4

Timing Information:

Preparation	Cooking	Total Time
5 mins	10 mins	15 mins

Nutritional Information:

Calories	508 kcal
Fat	33.9 g
Carbohydrates	35.1g
Protein	17.6 g
Cholesterol	74 mg
Sodium	848 mg

* Percent Daily Values are based on a 2,000 calorie diet.

PROVOLONE CILANTRO LIME GRILLED CHEESE

Ingredients

Pico de Gallo:

- 1 tomato, minced
- 1/2 white onion, minced
- 2 tbsps chopped fresh cilantro, or to taste (optional)
- 1/2 lime, juiced
- salt and ground black pepper to taste
- Sandwich:
- 3 tbsps softened butter, or as needed
- 10 slices white bread
- 10 slices provolone cheese

Directions

- Get a bowl, mix: pepper, tomato, salt, onion, lime, and cilantro.

- Layer the following on half of your bread pieces: 1 piece of provolone, spoonful of tomato mix, 1 more piece of provolone.
- Top with remaining pieces of bread to form sandwiches. Coat the outside of each sandwich with butter.
- Fry for 4 mins in a preheated pan.
- Enjoy.

Servings: 5

Timing Information:

Preparation	Cooking	Total Time
20 mins	20 mins	40 mins

Nutritional Information:

Calories	404 kcal
Fat	23.7 g
Carbohydrates	29.3g
Protein	18.8 g
Cholesterol	57 mg
Sodium	889 mg

* Percent Daily Values are based on a 2,000 calorie diet.

BROCCOLI PEPPER CHEDDAR GRILLED CHEESE

Ingredients

- 2 slices bread
- 2 slices Cheddar cheese
- 1/4 C. chopped broccoli
- 1/4 C. chopped zucchini
- 1/4 C. chopped green bell pepper
- 1 tbsp chopped jalapeno pepper
- 3 tbsps butter

Directions

- Get a frying pan hot with nonstick spray.
- Layer the following on a piece of bread: 1 piece of cheddar, bell pepper, broccoli, jalapeno, 1 piece of cheddar, and zucchini.
- Top with remaining piece of bread. Coat the outside of the sandwich with butter.

- Cook for 1 min per side in the frying pan, covered.
- Enjoy.

Servings: 1

Timing Information:

Preparation	Cooking	Total Time
10 mins	5 mins	15 mins

Nutritional Information:

Calories	689 kcal
Fat	55.2 g
Carbohydrates	30.6g
Protein	19.7 g
Cholesterol	151 mg
Sodium	950 mg

* Percent Daily Values are based on a 2,000 calorie diet.

PICKLE AND SWEET ONION GRILLED CHEESE

Ingredients

- 3 tbsps softened butter
- 2 slices whole wheat bread
- 2 slices sharp Cheddar cheese
- 1 dill pickle, sliced
- 2 thin slices Vidalia or other sweet onion

Directions

- Get a frying pan hot, before continuing.
- Coat one piece of bread with half your butter.
- Melt remaining butter in the pan then lay the un-buttered piece of bread into the frying pan. Top with cheddar, onions, and pickles. Put the buttered piece of bread on top of the pickled with

the buttered portion facing upwards.

- Cook for 5 mins. Then flip. Cook for another 5 mins.
- Enjoy.

Servings: 1

Timing Information:

Preparation	Cooking	Total Time
10 mins	5 mins	15 mins

Nutritional Information:

Calories	683 kcal
Fat	55.3 g
Carbohydrates	26.2g
Protein	22.1 g
Cholesterol	151 mg
Sodium	956 mg

* Percent Daily Values are based on a 2,000 calorie diet.

EASY SWISS WITH A TWIST GRILLED CHEESE

Ingredients

- 2 slices whole wheat bread
- 1 1/2 tsps olive oil
- 1/2 Granny Smith apple - peeled, cored and thinly sliced
- 1/3 C. shredded Swiss cheese

Directions

- Get a frying pan hot before doing anything else.
- Coat one piece of bread with olive oil. Then enter it into the frying pan with the oiled side facing downwards.
- Layer your apple, and then your cheese on the bread. Top with the other piece of bread. Then coat the top with some more olive oil.

- Cook for about 2 to 4 mins per side. Until you find that the cheese is completely melted.

Servings: 1

Timing Information:

Preparation	Cooking	Total Time
10 mins	5 mins	15 mins

Nutritional Information:

Calories	371 kcal
Fat	19 g
Carbohydrates	33.9g
Protein	17.3 g
Cholesterol	33 mg
Sodium	338 mg

* Percent Daily Values are based on a 2,000 calorie diet.

A Gift From Me To You...

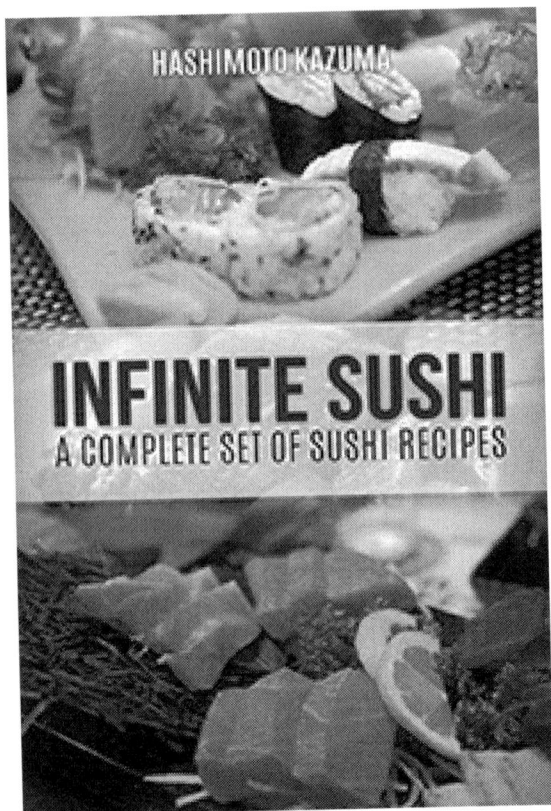

HASHIMOTO KAZUMA

INFINITE SUSHI
A COMPLETE SET OF SUSHI RECIPES

Send the Book!

I know you like easy cooking. But what about Japanese Sushi?

Join my private reader's club and get a copy of *__Infinite Sushi: A Complete Set of Sushi and Japanese Recipes__* by fellow BookSumo author Hashimoto Kazuma for FREE!

Send the Book!

Enjoy some of the best sushi available!

You will also receive updates about all my new books when they are free. So please show your support.

Also don't forget to like and subscribe on the social networks. I love meeting my readers. Links to all my profiles are below so please click and connect :)

Facebook

Twitter

COME ON...
LET'S BE FRIENDS :)

I adore my readers and love connecting with them socially. Please follow the links below so we can connect on Facebook, Twitter, and Google+.

Facebook

Twitter

I also have a blog that I regularly update for my readers so check it out below.

My Blog

CAN I ASK A FAVOUR?

If you found this book interesting, or have otherwise found any benefit in it. Then may I ask that you post a review of it on Amazon? Nothing excites me more than new reviews, especially reviews which suggest new topics for writing. I do read all reviews and I always factor feedback into my newer works.

So if you are willing to take ten minutes to write what you sincerely thought about this book then please visit our Amazon page and post your opinions.

Again thank you!

INTERESTED IN OTHER EASY COOKBOOKS?

Everything is easy! Check out my Amazon Author page for more great cookbooks:

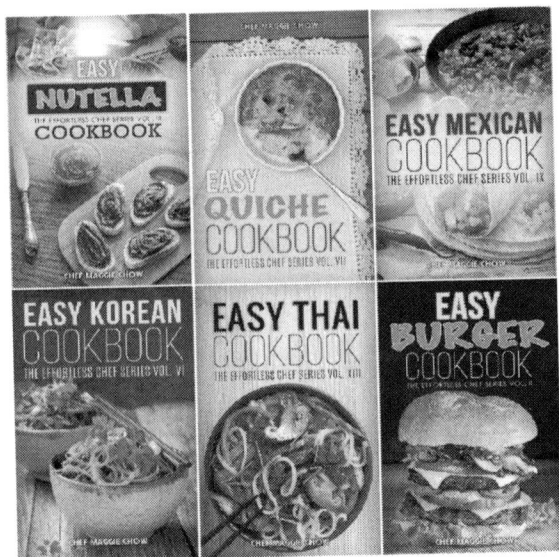

For a complete listing of all my books please see my author page.

Made in the USA
Lexington, KY
10 October 2018